W9-BZC-607

The Stock Market Crash of 1929

Sabrina Crewe and Scott Ingram

Gareth Stevens Publishing

A WORLD ALMANAC EDUCATION GROUP COMPANY

Please visit our web site at: www.garethstevens.com
For a free color catalog describing Gareth Stevens Publishing's list of high-quality
books and multimedia programs, call 1-800-542-2595 (USA) or 1-800-387-3178
(Canada). Gareth Stevens Publishing's fax: (414) 332-3567.

Library of Congress Cataloging-in-Publication Data

Crewe, Sabrina.
   The Stock market crash of 1929 / by Sabrina Crewe and Scott Ingram.
      p. cm. — (Events that shaped America)
   Includes bibliographical references and index.
   ISBN 0-8368-3416-X (lib. bdg.)
   1. Stock Market Crash, 1929—Juvenile literature.   2. Depressions—1929—
United States—Juvenile literature.   I. Ingram, Scott.   II. Title.   III. Series.
   HB37171929.C74   2005
   973.91'6—dc22   2004057128

This North American edition first published in 2005 by
Gareth Stevens Publishing
A WRC Media Company
330 West Olive Street, Suite 100
Milwaukee, WI 53212 USA

This edition © 2005 by Gareth Stevens Publishing.

Produced by Discovery Books
Editor: Sabrina Crewe
Designer and page production: Sabine Beaupré
Photo researcher: Sabrina Crewe
Maps and diagrams: Stefan Chabluk
Gareth Stevens editorial direction: Mark J. Sachner
Gareth Stevens editor: Monica Rausch
Gareth Stevens art direction: Tammy West
Gareth Stevens production: Jessica Morris

Photo credits: Corbis: cover, pp. 4, 5, 6, 7, 8, 9, 10, 11, 12, 13, 14, 15, 16, 17, 18, 21, 22, 23, 24, 25, 26, 27.

All rights reserved. No part of this book may be reproduced, stored in a retrieval system, or transmitted in any form or by any means, electronic, mechanical, photocopying, recording, or otherwise, without the prior written permission of the copyright holder.

Printed in the United States of America

1 2 3 4 5 6 7 8 9 09 08 07 06 05

Contents

Introduction

A Busy Day

Thursday, October 24, 1929, was a busy day at the New York **Stock** Exchange on Wall Street in Manhattan. The stock exchange was the financial center for American investors. For most of the 1920s, people with money to **invest** had been eagerly buying **shares** in large companies. If the companies made **profits**, the investors' shares rose in value.

Panic

By October 24, however, the value of most stocks had been falling for more than six weeks. That morning, the value of shares on the New York Stock Exchange dropped severely as soon as the market opened. As news spread, investors rushed to sell their shares and cut their losses. The huge rush to sell only caused the stock market to drop faster. On October 29, 1929—a day now known as "Black Tuesday"—the stock market collapsed.

This photo shows Wall Street in Manhattan in the early 1900s. Wall Street was New York City's business district and home to the United States' most important financial institutions.

The Stock Market

The stock market is, like any other market, a place for buying and selling. In the stock market, people buy and sell shares in company stock at places called stock exchanges.

If you buy a share in a company, you own a little piece of that company. So when that company makes money, you make money, too. If you own shares in a profitable company, you will receive money every year from the company's profits.

Prices of shares change all the time, depending on how well the company and the **economy** are doing. Some people make lots of money by buying shares at one price and selling them later when the price goes up. Buying shares on the stock market is always a gamble, however, because no one can be absolutely sure what will happen next.

Many families became jobless and homeless during the Great Depression. Like this family in Oklahoma, they moved around, hoping to find work.

The Crash and the Great Depression

The six-day period from October 24 to October 29, 1929, is known today as the stock market crash. It marked the beginning of one of the darkest periods in U.S. history. By early 1930, businesses and banks across the country had failed. By 1932, one of every four American workers was jobless. The Great **Depression** gripped the nation.

Chapter One
The Roaring Twenties

Rows of mass-produced Model T Fords sit in an automobile factory in the 1920s. By 1925, a Model T rolled off the Ford assembly line every ten seconds.

Nuts and Bolts of Production

"To do his work [a man] must have every second necessary but not a single unnecessary second . . . the man who puts in a bolt does not put on the nut; the man who puts on the nut does not tighten it."

Henry Ford, explaining the division of labor on his assembly line

The Decade of the Automobile
The 1920s were known as the "Roaring Twenties" because of the way life got "faster" and more exciting. Many changes occurred, but the most important change was that many people began using cars. The government built highways for cars, and soon gas stations, motels, and roadside restaurants sprang up across the nation.

Assembly Lines
The automobile changed everyday life, and it changed industry, too. An important person behind this change was Henry Ford, who was determined to build cars as cheaply and quickly as possible. He developed a system called the assembly line. Each worker in Ford's factory did just one job, from welding a part of the car's frame to filling the radiator with water. Workers stood in one place while a conveyor belt carried the vehicles past them.

Modern Conveniences and Prosperity

Soon, other industries across the United States adopted assembly lines. U.S. companies began turning out new appliances such as radios, refrigerators, and washing machines in large numbers. Before long, these **mass-produced** items became part of almost every household.

New Kinds of Entertainment

In the 1920s, many new inventions brought amusements Americans had never even imagined. Mass entertainment, in the form of radio and movies, grew popular in the 1920s. People would gather around radios for their favorite shows, and millions flocked to movie theaters every week. New forms of music also became a big part of life in the 1920s. Jazz, born in the African-American communities of the South, moved into the big cities of the North. Jazz clubs sprang up, and dance crazes such as the Charleston roared across the country.

A poster advertises a Charlie Chaplin movie in the 1920s.

In the 1920s, most people did not earn enough to buy all the new and exciting products they wanted. Poorer families bought radios, like the one these boys are listening to, and other appliances on credit.

Buying on Credit

The cost of all the exciting new products, however, was often more than a family could afford. In order to keep up sales, companies began to sell products on credit. Under this arrangement, customers made a first payment, called a "down payment," on an item and took it home. They promised to pay the rest of the cost over a period of time, plus an additional sum as **interest**.

Selling goods to customers on credit made many companies profitable in the first half of the 1920s. As a result, those companies made more and more products—workers churned out 40 percent more goods in 1925 than they made in 1920. Workers' wages, however, increased just 8 percent during that time. So although there were more and more goods, there were few customers with enough money to buy them.

Helping Business Owners

Calvin Coolidge, who was president from 1923 to 1929, worked to keep the manufacturing companies free of high

taxes and government controls, which helped to make some business owners very rich. There were no laws to make companies pay decent wages or keep their factories safe. Profits were high, therefore, and business owners kept nearly all their profits because of the low taxes.

Economic Inequality

In the 1920s, a wealthy minority had enough money to keep buying what the factories produced, and so the economy looked good. Beneath the explosion of production and buying, however, were some disturbing facts. Almost three-fourths of American families had to spend their entire incomes on basic needs, such as food, clothing, and housing. Many people struggled with debt.

The benefits of the so-called "Coolidge Prosperity," therefore, were limited to a small percentage of the wealthiest Americans. In 1926, the richest 0.1 percent of Americans had a combined income equal to the poorest 42 percent of Americans. An example of this inequality was Henry Ford. He earned $14 million in 1927, when the average income was only about $1,000 a year.

Changing Times
"The man who builds a factory, builds a temple. The man who works there, worships there."

President Calvin Coolidge, 1926

The **federal** government encouraged farmers in the 1920s to borrow money to buy tractors and other modern equipment so they could produce more food. The farmers were soon in debt.

Chapter Two

The Stock Market

Bright Future

"Ours is a land rich in resources . . . filled with millions of happy homes, blessed with comfort and opportunity. . . . I have no fears for the future. . . . It is bright with hope."

Herbert Hoover, during his inauguration as U.S. president, March 1929

Belief in the Stock Market

In spite of widespread poverty, the United States appeared to be prospering. For five years—from 1924 to 1929—the value of shares on the stock market had been rising rapidly. The rise seemed to show a healthy growth in the economy and in the value of the nation's businesses. What it really reflected, however, was the fact that lots of people were buying shares in the hope of getting rich.

Between 1927 and 1929, the whole country seemed to be trying to get rich by investing in the stock market. Thousands of small investors followed the prices of shares, including these two visitors to the New York Stock Exchange in 1929.

Hopeful Investors

During the 1920s, investors were eager to buy any stock, and many companies in the 1920s made enormous amounts of money from the sale of shares. Some of this money was invested in building new factories, buying new machines, and hiring more workers. This investment led, in turn, to greater production of goods.

American industries were soon producing far more goods than they could sell. They were still selling shares to eager investors, who believed the stock would increase in value. If the companies weren't selling all of their goods, however, they weren't making profits. The shares, therefore, weren't worth as much as people thought. Sooner or later, that fact would cause a serious problem.

Buying on Margin

There was another problem building up. Many people who invested in the stock market did not have enough money to buy shares of stock, so they paid a little bit and borrowed the remaining money from the **brokers** who were selling them the stock. This practice is called "buying on **margin**." The brokers charged the investors the cost of the stock plus a fee.

Buying on margin worked well as long as stock prices continued to rise, and many investors were buying shares that way. The brokers, meanwhile, were borrowing the money from banks to lend to the investors to buy the shares. So, if a stock suddenly lost its value, there would be a chain of debt with just some worthless stock at the end of it. Unfortunately, the people doing the lending and borrowing weren't thinking too hard about that possibility.

Take it wherever you go!

UNDER a tree, on a mountain top—tune in. Out on the sea, lazing coolly on the deck—tune in! And off for a motor trip, put into the car one more suitcase—a Radiola Super-Heterodyne *complete*. Its loudspeaker is built-in, its loop in the cover, its batteries inside!

The Radiola Super-Heterodyne is made, now, in two portable models. It is the same far-famed "Super-Het"—with the same fine quality of tone—the same complete simplicity —the same distance performance. But it is portable now —and you can take your entertainment with you everywhere!

Radio Corporation of America

Chicago — New York — San Francisco

Radiola
REG. U.S. PAT. OFF. RCA
PRODUCED ONLY BY RCA

Radiola 24
Built in a suitcase of black cowhide, cobra grain. Open ready for use. And closed for carrying. With 6 Radiotrons UV-199 - - - $195

Radiola 26
Finished in Walnut. Complete for carrying. And with an extra battery cabinet for home use. With 6 Radiotrons UV-199 - - - $225

People invested in rapidly growing companies such as the Radio Corporation of America (RCA). When RCA stock shot up in value, investors felt rich, even if were really in debt from buying on margin.

Clerks in a brokers' office near Wall Street read the latest prices on the **ticker tape**. When the stock market was busy, stock prices changed constantly.

The Federal Reserve Board

A few people however, were watching and worrying. The **Federal Reserve** Board was an official group that kept an eye on the nation's banks and helped them when they needed it. Board members were alarmed by the enormous amounts of money that banks had loaned to brokers so people could buy on margin. Members of the Federal Reserve Board feared that any drop in stock value would make investors unable to repay brokers. Brokers then would not be able to repay banks, and the nation's banking system would be put at risk.

Raising Interest Rates

The board decided to raise **interest rates**. This rise would make it more expensive for people to borrow money, and the board hoped the cycle of borrowing and buying would then slow down. But American investors went on buying stocks with little or no understanding of their value. The stock market continued to rise throughout the summer of 1929.

Fools Get Rich

"People who know the least about the stock market have made the most money out of it in the last few months. Fools who rushed in where wise men feared to tread ran up high gains."

The New York Times, *March 24, 1929*

Ignoring the Problems

The average investors were not the only people who did not understand the growing threat. Financial experts had also become convinced that the rising stock market meant all was well with the U.S. economy. They weren't looking at the real signs, however, such as new house construction, sales of goods, workers' wages, or how the banks were doing. By any of these measures, the economy was actually beginning to slow down.

Early Warning

In 1928, banker Charles Merrill (left) was very uneasy about the state of the stock market. He appealed to President Coolidge to speak out against reckless borrowing and stock buying. Coolidge ignored Merrill's pleas. By February 1929, Merrill was so certain that the stock market was headed for collapse that he sold all of his stock and advised his customers to pull their money out of the market. Widely criticized for his decision in February, Merrill became a celebrity when his prediction came true in October.

Chapter Three

The Crash

Falling Prices

At last, in early September 1929, the problems started to show. Stocks began to lose value as companies reported falling sales and low profits. This downward movement continued, and on Monday, October 21, prices suddenly dropped across the market.

The New York Stock Exchange

The New York Stock Exchange in the 1920s.

The New York Stock Exchange (NYSE) is not the only stock exchange in the United States, but it is the oldest and biggest. The exchange opened in 1817 and, in 1903, moved to the building on Wall Street that it occupies today. In 1929, most of the daily activity took place on a huge trading floor inside the NYSE. Every day, trading opened and closed at the sound of a loud bell. On the floor were more than five hundred horseshoe-shaped trading desks, one for each company that offered stock for sale. Brokers, representing large and small investors, shouted orders and gathered around ticker tape machines. Through the crowds and confusion, many messengers and tickertape boys dashed around, carrying orders and stock updates.

Black Thursday

At the opening bell on Thursday, October 24, the New York Stock Exchange became a beehive of activity. Prices were falling, and investors were trying to sell their shares because they didn't want to lose more money than they already had lost. Brokers pushed and shoved around trading desks where the action was heaviest—those at which the shares of the largest companies, such as General Electric and U.S. Steel, were traded.

Huge numbers of orders to sell shares were coming into the stock exchange, causing the prices of stock to change minute by minute. The ticker tape machine couldn't keep up with the changes.

Technical Condition

"There has been a little distress selling on the Stock Exchange . . . due to a technical condition of the market."

Broker Thomas Lamont of Morgan Investments, addressing reporters, Thursday, October 24, 1929

On October 24, small investors were the ones hit the hardest by the drop in stock prices. This group waited nervously outside the NYSE for news of their investments.

Police officers on horseback were called in to control the crowds gathering on Wall Street in October 1929.

The Panic Begins

Worried investors across the country, unable to learn the latest price changes, began to panic and tried to sell their shares. They tried to call brokers in the stock exchange itself, but the lines were busy.

Meanwhile, people gathered outside the exchanges and brokerages, and police were dispatched to ensure peace. By late morning, crowds of investors were trying to force their way inside the New York Stock Exchange to contact their brokers. Police were called to control rioting by some of the wealthiest people in American business.

Pooling Resources

At lunchtime on October 24, the most powerful bankers and brokers in New York City gathered. The only way to avoid a massive stock market collapse, they agreed, was to buy shares.

By early afternoon, they had pooled more than $30 million of their own money and started buying shares.

By the end of the day that came to be known as "Black Thursday," the losses of the morning had been stopped. Nevertheless, the fall on Thursday basically wiped out the small investors—those who owned fewer than five thousand shares of stock.

The Small Investors

By 1929, many people had invested in the stock market who could not afford the risk. Individual investors, although they lost smaller amounts, were hit hard because they had bought on margin. People not only sold their stock, but they sold cars, jewelry, even their homes, to try and meet their debts to their brokers. If the money was not there when the broker demanded it, the stock would be sold, and the investor would have nothing left except a debt to the broker.

Nothing Left
"The first day of October in 1929 made me feel like I was rich [but after the crash] I was wiped out. . . . I had nothing left."

George Mehales, Greek immigrant who lost his business and all his money because of the 1929 stock market crash

$100. WILL BUY THIS CAR. MUST HAVE CASH LOST ALL ON THE STOCK MARKET

Suddenly, people who thought they were rich had nothing. This investor, wiped out by his losses, tried to raise cash by selling his luxury car at a bargain price.

Clerks on Wall Street worked long hours without sleep, trying to keep up with changing prices and customers' orders.

Black Monday

President Herbert Hoover (who had taken over from Coolidge in March 1929) addressed the nation on Friday, October 25. He tried to reassure Americans, saying that the economy was fine. The selling, however, continued. Over the weekend, people on Wall Street kept working night and day to try and catch up with all the activity.

An hour after the opening bell on Monday, October 28, it became clear that the market was still headed down. Panic selling broke out again. Investors who could not buy enough shares several months earlier now could not sell their shares fast enough. On Black Monday, the market lost more than 12 percent of its value, far worse than on the previous Thursday.

Vanished Hopes

"Wall Street was a street of vanished hopes, of curiously silent apprehension and of a sort of paralyzed hypnosis yesterday. Men and women crowded the brokerage offices, even those who have been long since wiped out, and followed the figures on the tape."

The New York Times, *October 30, 1929*

Black Tuesday

The crash of Black Monday largely ruined wealthy people, large banks, and giant investment houses. The next day, Tuesday, October 29, was even worse. At the opening bell, the trading floor of the NYSE was eerily quiet.

Within a few hours, prices fell so low that all of the financial gains of the previous year were lost. Millions of investors and brokers were completely wiped out. The stock market had simply collapsed.

The Dow Jones Index

The Dow Jones index is a useful guide to the price of shares. A change in the Dow Jones figure from one day to the next shows that the average price of shares on the index has risen or fallen. In 1929, the Dow Jones based its daily figure on the price of stock in thirty leading U.S. companies, such as U.S. Steel and Radio Corporation of America. This chart shows what happened to the value of shares before, during, and after the stock market crash of 1929, as reflected by the Dow Jones index.

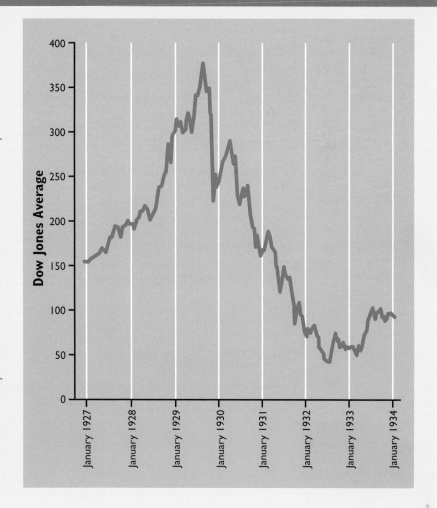

Chapter Four

The Great Depression

After the Crash

Some effects of the stock market crash were immediate. Business owners watched the worth of their companies vanish overnight. Stockbrokers were ruined when investors could not pay back the money they owed from buying on margin. Many investors lost everything they had. Above all, the crash caused people to lose confidence in the nation's economy.

The Economy in Ruins

Other consequences soon followed. Large and small companies began to lay off workers and close factories when sales of their goods dropped. The Great Depression had begun.

Banks, too, were hurt by the rapidly worsening economy. Those banks that had loaned money to brokers and investors

By July 1932, with the United States in the grip of the Great Depression, share prices hit their lowest point. The prices of shares in some of the largest U.S. companies dropped way below even the lowest levels reached during the days of the crash.

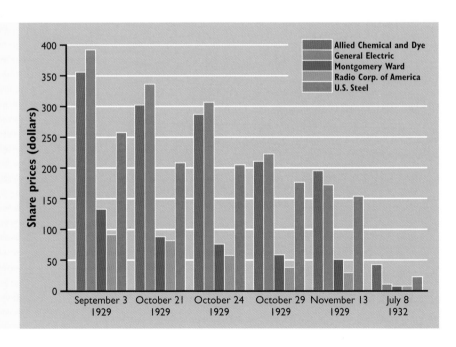

A Hooverville in Seattle, Washington.

During the Great Depression, thousands of Americans who once had houses and jobs became homeless. They began to build huts on vacant lots in cities and suburbs. The huts were made of scrap metal, wood, cardboard, or anything else that could be found in dumps. These towns for the homeless became known as "Hoovervilles" because people blamed President Hoover for the Depression. Hoovervilles were without electricity, plumbing, or water. The people who lived in them had no money to buy food or medicine, and many were starving and sick.

found themselves short of funds. By the end of 1930, more than four thousand banks had failed. People who had saved for years to buy a home or educate their children had their dreams shattered when they lost their bank savings. Older Americans who planned to use their savings for retirement suddenly found themselves penniless.

Depression on the Farms

The Great Depression hit everyone, but it was worse for Americans in rural areas. By 1929, low crop prices meant farmers could not make their loan payments to banks. Between 1930 and 1932, one million families lost their farms.

When it seemed things could not get any worse, one of the worst **droughts** in history hit the nation in the 1930s. On farms from Tennessee to Oklahoma, in an area that became known as the Dust Bowl, crops failed and livestock died.

Unemployed veterans of World War I, called the "Bonus Army," marched to Washington, D.C., and camped there in 1932 to ask for bonuses they were owed. Hoover called out the U.S. Army to drive the veterans out of town.

Homeless and Hungry

During President Hoover's term, the average weekly wage of workers had fallen from $25 to $17. Yet those who earned wages were the lucky ones. About one in every four workers in the United States was without a job.

Millions of people were homeless and hungry. Every day, local charities fed thousands of people who stood in line for hours to get a free meal. About two out of every three children in New York City were sick because they did not have enough food to eat.

Vigorous Action
"We do not distrust the future of democracy . . . the people of the United States . . . want direct, vigorous action."

Franklin D. Roosevelt, inaugural address, March 1933

The Election of 1932

By 1932, the U.S. faced the worst economic crisis in its history. In the presidential election that year, American voters totally rejected the ideas of President Hoover and former President Coolidge, who said that the government should not regulate business or help people who lost their jobs. The voters chose instead the Democratic candidate for president, Franklin D. Roosevelt, who promised Americans the New Deal, a group of federal programs to help farmers and workers.

Roosevelt Takes Over

After taking office in March 1933, Roosevelt's first major action was to declare a national bank holiday and close all the banks. He declared that only banks whose records passed federal inspection would be allowed to reopen. By mid-summer, more than three-fourths of the banks in the nation were open again, and the American people once again felt safe depositing their money in banks.

Regulating the Market

After the bank holiday, Roosevelt created the Securities and Exchange Commission (SEC) to oversee the stock market. The SEC was given the power to make sure that the price of stocks was fair and the people who sold them were honest. The Federal Reserve Board would keep a watch over buying on margin, too. The risky practice would be controlled so it wouldn't get out of hand again.

By the time Roosevelt became president, people were desperate for jobs. In this photo, unemployed men lined up outside a soup kitchen in Chicago that gave out free food.

Thousands of WPA employees worked on highways and city streets under the New Deal. These workers were widening a road to allow for automobile traffic.

Work for the People

As he had promised with the New Deal, Roosevelt formed federal agencies to help Americans back to work. The Civilian Conservation Corps (CCC) provided jobs in rural areas. CCC workers planted trees, stocked rivers with fish, and cleared wilderness trails in national parks and forests.

Next came the Public Works Administration (PWA) and Civil Works Administration (CWA), which hired Americans to build schools, hospitals, and housing and improve parks and roads. In 1935, most employment programs were combined under the Works Progress Administration (WPA). WPA workers built highways, dams, bridges, and public buildings. In addition, the WPA employed writers, artists, actors, and musicians. They wrote guidebooks, painted murals on government buildings, and gave public performances.

A Popular President

President Roosevelt's opponents claimed that he made the federal government too powerful. The American public, however, solidly supported the president, and he was reelected in 1936. Roosevelt broke the presidential tradition of serving only two terms and ran successfully in 1940 and again in 1944.

Roosevelt wasn't able to solve all the grim economic problems, but he did restore Americans' trust in government and business. As a result, people's faith in the economy slowly returned. The economy did not truly recover, however, until the United States entered World War II in 1941.

Franklin Delano Roosevelt (1882–1945)

A 1938 cartoon shows President Roosevelt in the middle of a group of children who symbolize the New Deal programs.

Franklin D. Roosevelt came from a wealthy New York family. After training as a lawyer, Roosevelt entered politics at a young age, becoming a state senator in New York before the age of thirty.

In 1921, Roosevelt was stricken with polio and was eventually unable to walk. In 1928, he was elected governor of New York, and in 1932 he won the U.S. presidential election. Roosevelt was a strong and popular leader determined to help Americans through the Great Depression.

He went on to lead the nation through its next great crisis, when the United States entered World War II in 1941. Roosevelt died soon after being elected for the fourth time. He was the only president ever elected to four terms.

Conclusion

The Impact of the Crash

The stock market crash of 1929 caused a huge change to take place in the United States. Until then, people had faith in the stock market and believed that business should be free of government controls. Unsuspecting investors bought worthless stocks, hoping to get rich. Meanwhile, the economy was falling apart, and no one was doing anything about it. The crash, when it came, made many people poor. It also created doubt and mistrust in banks, businesses, and the stock market. The United States took many years to recover from the results of the crash.

Because of the 1929 crash, certain safeguards were introduced into the U.S. financial world. Prices of shares may rise and fall, but the U.S. economy—and the stock market itself—is protected against collapse.

In the 1930s and 1940s, the government displayed posters to introduce Americans to the new programs of the Roosevelt years. For the first time, the federal government offered pensions for retired people and **welfare** programs for the sick and unemployed.

Roosevelt's Legacy

Another protection that Americans still enjoy came from the years after the stock market crash. During his second term, President Roosevelt put in place many government programs that are taken for granted in modern American life. The support that citizens receive from the government today—whether they are sick, unemployed, veterans of wars, or retired—started in Roosevelt's time.

The Stock Market Today

Today, the New York Stock Exchange is housed in the same building as it was in October 1929. With new technology, investors from around the world can contact brokers in New York to buy and sell shares within seconds. The U.S. economy has become much more intertwined with the world's economy, and many factors now affect the price of shares at the NYSE.

One thing, however, is the same: As in 1929, investing in the stock market is a risky business. Even so, more Americans are investing in the stock market now than ever before.

The trading floor of the New York Stock Exchange is even busier today than it was in 1929. Today, ticker tapes and messengers have been replaced by computers and cell phones providing instant information.

Time Line

1817   New York Stock Exchange is founded.

1896   Dow Jones index is created.

1903   New York Stock Exchange moves to current home on Wall Street.

1913   Federal Reserve Bank system is created.
         Henry Ford opens automobile manufacturing factory.

1928   Herbert Hoover is elected president.

1929   March: Federal Reserve Board raises interest rates.
         September 3: Stocks begin to decline.
         October 24: Black Thursday.
         October 28: Black Monday.
         October 29: Black Tuesday.
         Great Depression begins.

1930   Banks begin to fail across United States.
         Beginning of Dust Bowl conditions in the Midwest.

1932   Franklin D. Roosevelt is elected president.

1933   March: President Roosevelt declares national bank holiday for federal bank inspection.
         New Deal programs reorganize the banking system and set up government-sponsored projects to employ millions.

1936   Roosevelt is elected to second term.

1939   World War II begins.

1940   Roosevelt is elected to third term.

1941   United States enters World War II.
         Great Depression ends.

Things to Think About and Do

Investing on the Stock Market

Look for stock reports in a newspaper or on the Internet, and choose a company that sells its stock on the New York Stock Exchange. Pretend you have bought twenty shares of stock in that company. Follow the ups and downs in the price of your shares for a few weeks by checking the daily or weekly listings.

Living through the Great Depression

Find out more about the Great Depresson and how it affected families and farms in the Dust Bowl region. Imagine you are a member of a farming family from the region, and write an account of some of your experiences in the Great Depression.

Glossary

broker: person who buys and sells things on behalf of another person. A broker who buys and sells shares is called a stockbroker.

depression: long period of time when the economy slows down, jobs are lost, and people stop spending money.

drought: period with much less rainfall than usual, causing shortages of water.

economy: system of producing and distributing goods and services.

federal: having to do with national government.

interest: amount of extra money paid back on a borrowed sum of money.

interest rate: percentage of interest charged on loans or paid out on savings. Bank interest rates go up and down according to the rate set by the U.S. government.

invest: put money into something in the hope of making more money.

margin: part payment made on shares, with the rest to be paid later.

mass-produced: made in large numbers in a factory.

profit: gain made by a business or person after all expenses are paid.

reserve: amount kept aside or held back for a special reason, such as a sudden shortage or other emergency.

share: one of a number of equal parts into which a company's stock can be divided. The value of the share goes up and down according to the wealth and success of the company.

stock: value, or wealth, of a company.

tax: sum charged by the government on purchases or income and used to pay for public services or the cost of governing.

ticker tape: paper tape that prints out information sent to tickers, which are machines that receive information through telegraph wires.

welfare: help provided by government programs for people in need.

Further Information

Books

Graves, Kerry A. *Going to School During the Great Depression*. Capstone, 2001.

Maupin, Melissa. *Franklin D. Roosevelt: Our Thirty-Second President* (Our Presidents). Child's World, 2001.

Whitcraft, Melissa. *Wall Street* (Cornerstones of Freedom). Children's Press, 2003.

Woolf, Alex. *The Wall Street Crash, October 29, 1929* (Days that Shook the World). Raintree, 2002.

Web Sites

www.newdeal.feri.org Educational guide to the Great Depression from the Franklin and Eleanor Roosevelt Institute.

www.nyse.com New York Stock Exchange Web site has current news, history, and information about how the stock market works.

www.prongo.com/stock Children's educational Web site allows you to find the price of a company's stock and track its changes.

www.sec.gov/about/whatwedo.shtml Web site of the U.S. Securities and Exchange Commission explains how the commission works and the laws that protect investors and the market.

Useful Addresses

New York Stock Exchange
11 Wall Street
New York, NY 10005
Telephone: (212) 656-3000

Index

JAN 07 MIL